Giants
Fishbones and Chocolate

Michael O'Reilly • Caroline Quinn

Skills Book

Carole by Carole Greene

Carroll Heinemann

Contents

Carroll Heinemann
Units 17-18
Willow Road Business Park
Knockmitten Lane
Dublin 12

Text © Michael O'Reilly, Caroline Quinn, 2001
Managing Editor: Gabrielle Jacob
Design: Artistix, Thame, Oxon
Illustrations: Stephanie Strickland

First published July 2001

ISBN 1 903574 13 7

The Diary of a Killer Cat

Before You Read: Talk About

1. Look at the title. What do you think a killer cat is?
2. Who wrote *The Diary of a Killer Cat*? Have you read any other story by her? Tell the class what the story was about.
3. Can you think of an animal that would not be suitable to keep as a pet? Say why you feel it would not suit. Make up a funny story about such a pet.
4. List words that could be used to describe cats e.g. sleek.

After You Read: Talk About

A.
1. How did Tuffy kill the bird?
2. (a) What did Tuffy do with the dead bird?
   (b) What did Ellie do with the dead bird?
3. What did Tuffy do (a) on Monday, (b) on Tuesday, (c) on Wednesday?
4. List some of the things that Tuffy does in the garden.
5. Why did Tuffy want to watch the bird's funeral?
6. Why did Ellie's mother "fetch sheets of old newspaper"?

B.
1. Did you like this story? Why?
2. Was Ellie kind-hearted? Why?
3. Why was the house turning into "Fun City"?
4. What did Ellie mean by saying "it's natural"?
5. Tell the story from the point of view of Ellie's father.
6. What tells you that Ellie's parents weren't cat lovers?
7. Did Tuffy regret what he had done? How do we know?
8. What do you think will happen next?

▶▶ Moving On

Draw a cartoon picture of Tuffy. Scan the story again and add Tuffy's thoughts to your drawing in thought bubbles.

Dictionary Dinosaurs 1

A. Here is a list of words from *The Diary of a Killer Cat*. Find the meanings in your dictionary and write them down.

biff _____

anemones _____

fetch _____

precious _____

pity _____

grateful _____

complain _____

hiss _____

B. Put the list of words in alphabetical order.

1. _____   2. _____

3. _____   4. _____

5. _____   6. _____

7. _____   8. _____

C. Write a short piece using some of these words.

My _____

_____

_____

_____

_____

_____

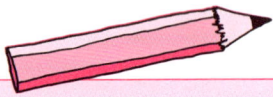

Verbs

A verb is an _____ _____. It tells us about an action.

A. Scan the story and list some of the verbs you find.

_____	_____
_____	_____
_____	_____
_____	_____
_____	_____
_____	_____
_____	_____

B. Choose a suitable verb for the following sentences.

1. The bee _____ happily from flower to flower.

2. A small boy _____ through the window of the shop.

3. Old Maisie _____ wearily up the hill.

4. Four robbers _____ away from the bank in a black car.

5. Our teacher looked around and suddenly he _____.

6. Dinosaurs _____ many years ago.

7. I _____ and _____ but could not escape the giant.

8. The horse _____ down the road and _____ over the gate.

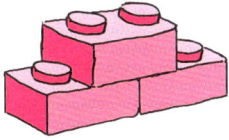

Tired Words 1

A. Sometimes, when we are writing, we use the verb *said* too often. Brainstorm other words that could be used instead of *said*.

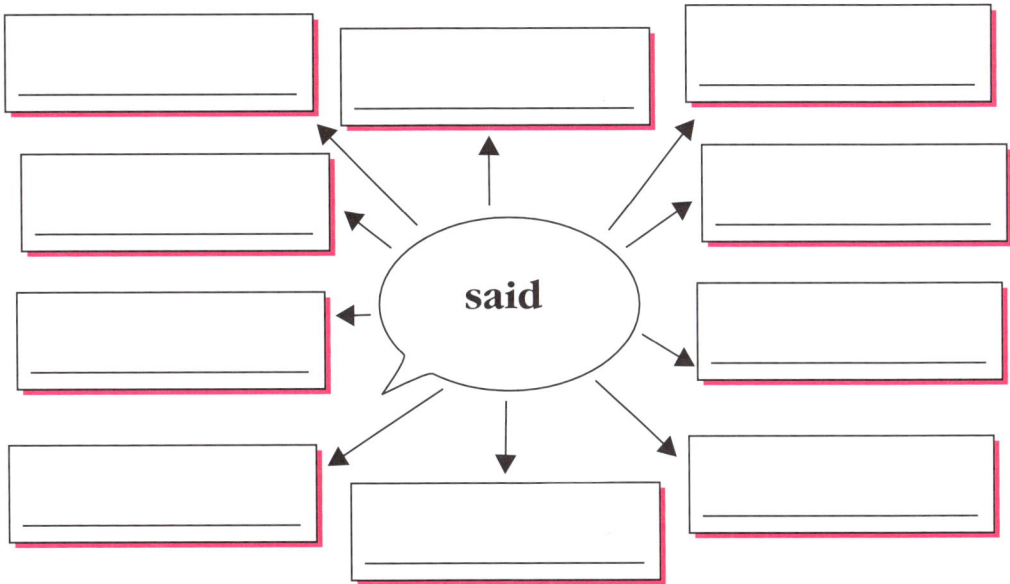

Add these words to your class word bank. Remember to check your word bank when you are writing.

B. Now make your own word banks for these verbs.

looked

ate

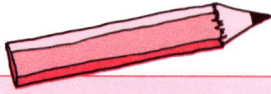

Nouns

A. Examine the first page of the story and find the nouns that follow these adjectives.

old _____   soapy _____   one _____

little _____   great _____   red _____

B. Examine the story and list all the nouns you find.

People	Places	Things

C. Edit and rewrite the following sentences giving each proper noun a capital letter.

1. My friends are called ann and john.
2. I would love to visit new york.
3. The river lee is long and winding.
4. The family were cross with tuffy the cat.
5. People sail on lough derg.
6. Children get lots of treats at christmas and easter.
7. We watch bart simpson on television.
8. The months of winter are november, december and january.

Ellie's Diary

In *The Diary of a Killer Cat* we read Tuffy's account of what happened.
Now write Ellie's account of what happened and how she felt.

Monday _____

_____

_____

_____

_____

Tuesday _____

_____

_____

_____

_____

Wednesday _____

_____

_____

_____

_____

Word Trap 1

A. Rewrite the sentences using the correct word.

1. Dad brought _____ dog to the vet.

2. Turn _____ the TV please.

3. The lion is called the king _____ beasts.

4. There _____ many different tribes living in the rainforests.

5. Where _____ _____ books? They _____ on the table.

B. Write sentences, falling into the traps on purpose. Give them to the person beside you to solve.

10

How Night Came to the World

Before You Read: Talk About

1. Every country has its own traditional stories. List some Irish traditional stories and retell one of them.

2. The Amazon is one of the greatest rivers in the world. What is the longest river? List some other great rivers. Use an atlas to help you.

3. What do you know about rainforests? Describe them. List some of the creatures that live there.

After You Read: Talk About

A. 1. (a) Why could the husband not sleep?
      (b) What did he do when he couldn't sleep?

   2. Who was sent to find the Great Snake?

   3. Describe the Great Snake.

   4. (a) What did the Great Snake bring from the river?
      (b) What did she say about it?

   5. What happened when the wax was scratched away?

   6. What happened to the boys?

B. 1. List some of the creatures named in this story.

   2. Was the daughter very clever? Why?

   3. Why were there "broken canoes" and "chewed bones" in the Great Snake's cave?

   4. Tell the story from the point of view of (a) the Great Snake, (b) the first boy.

   5. Summarise the main points of the story.

   6. Would you like to live in a world where there is only day? Why?

▶▶ Moving On

Do you know what causes day and night? Draw a diagram to show this. Find out more in your encyclopaedia or on the Internet.

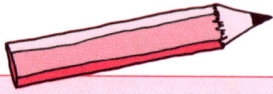

Sentences

A. Write the following sentences correctly.

1. ellie cried after the death of the bird

2. i enjoyed the bird's funeral

3. all i know is i found it

4. the cat ruined the flower beds

5. ellie's father was rude to tuffy

6. ellie put the bird in a box and buried it

B. Redraft and edit this following piece from *How Night Came to the World*. Don't look at your book until you have finished.

the cave was deep and damp all around were scattered broken canoes and

_____

chewed bones and there sleeping at the very back of the cave was the great

_____

snake her teeth were as long as a man's arm the boys came so close they

_____

could fell the snake's breath warm on their faces

_____

| **Final draft** _____ |
| _____ |
| _____ |
| _____ |

Words from Other Languages

A. Sometimes when stories come from other parts of the world, they contain strange words that do not have a matching word in English. There are three such words in this story. Unscramble them.

jubicum   hinmuba   ãmctuu

_____   _____   _____

B. We use many words from other languages every day. Can you solve these words?

1. Modelling material made from paper and glue

   p_____ m_____

2. A curved stick used in Australia

   b_____

3. An Irish drum

   b_____

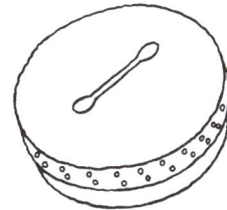

4. Stringy food from Italy

   s_____

5. An Inuit's home

   i_____

6. An Irish word for a dance

   c_____

7. A place to have lunch

   c_____

8. An Inuit word for a winter jacket

   a_____

9. A food from Italy with a bread base and cheese and tomato toppings

   p_____

15

Girl in Goal

Before You Read: Talk About

1. Look at the title of this story. Does it make you want to read the story?
2. What is your favourite sport? Why?
3. What is your favourite team? Talk about it.
4. List ten words that you think might be in the story.
5. What do you know about soccer? Read about it on page 8 of *Tyrannosaurus Sue*.

After You Read: Talk About

A. 1. Why did Ben not want Sam to play soccer?
   2. Why did Gareth say that Gateway were the "strongest team"?
   3. Why was Nozza like Ben?
   4. What did Gareth promise Jack if he managed to score?
   5. Why did Gareth tell Sam "to bring her cap"? Did the plan work?
   6. Why did Gareth ask Sam to play football?

B. 1. Did Gareth like Ben? How do we know?
   2. Was Sam the kind of girl to give up easily? How do we know?
   3. What words tell you that Mr Norris knew what was going on all the time?
   4. Who is your favourite character in the story? Why do you say so?
   5. What do you think happened next?
   6. Tell the story from the point of view of (a) Mr Norris, (b) Ben.
   7. Summarise the main points of the story.
   8. Is it right that some games should be played only by boys? Have a class debate.

▶▶ Moving On

What are the names of the children in the story? Draw a picture of each of them and choose words to describe her/him.

16

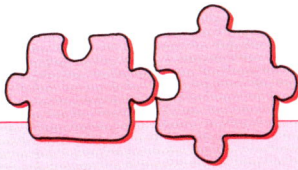

Compound Words

A. Join the words in these two lists to make new words.

fire	press
whirl	knife
hail	apple
pine	pecker
pen	works
wood	pool
hot	stone

B. Examine the story again and list the compound words you find.

O _____   _____

O _____   _____

O _____   _____

O _____   _____

C. Write out the two words that make up each of the compound words above.

O _____/_____   _____/_____

O _____/_____   _____/_____

O _____/_____   _____/_____

O _____/_____   _____/_____

Past and Present 1

Look at these verbs.

Today: **wash**   **bake**

Yesterday: **washed**   **baked**

The words **baked** and **washed** are in the past tense. We add **-d** or **-ed** to many verbs to form the past tense.

Example

I **wash** myself every morning.

I **washed** myself yesterday morning.

A. Look at the verbs in the first box. Find their past tense in the second box.

smile	closed
open	lived
close	smiled
cook	looked
live	opened
look	cooked

B. Now write the following sentences in the past tense.

1. I watch television on Sunday.

2. Every day, I walk to school.

3. I stay in bed late on Saturday.

4. The lifeguard saves drowning people at the beach.

5. Eoin and Sarah love the circus.

6. Sam plays football everyday.

C. Write sentences in the present tense. Swap them with the person beside you and rewrite their sentences in the past tense.

Now look at these verbs. You must double the last letter and add **-ed** to make the past tense.

Example

rub   rub**bed**

D. Can you make the past tense of these verbs?

hop _____   hip _____

chop _____   hob _____

bob _____   lap _____

stop _____   pat _____

fit _____   fret _____

E. Can you think of six more verbs like these?

○ _____   _____

○ _____   _____

○ _____   _____

F. Examine the first page of the story. List all the verbs you find that are in the past tense.

○ _____   _____

○ _____   _____

○ _____   _____

○ _____   _____

○ _____   _____

○ _____   _____

○ _____   _____

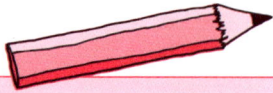

Extending a Sentence 1

Sometimes we write boring sentences. By adding more information to our sentences, we can make them more interesting. We can do this by answering questions.

Example

Sam was sad. **Why?**

Sam was sad **because she was not allowed to play football**.

A. **Extend these sentences by answering the questions.**

1. Gateway hadn't won any matches. (Why?)

   _____

2. The trees swayed in the breeze. (Why? and When?)

   _____

3. Dad's car broke down. (Why? and When? and Where?)

   _____

4. The bird flew away. (Where? and Why? and When?)

   _____

5. Our teacher was annoyed. (Why? and When?)

   _____

B. **Now extend these sentences in your own way.**

1. Ellie's father hated cats.
2. Tuffy wanted to watch the bird's funeral.
3. The village chief's son couldn't sleep.
4. The Great Snake's daughter turned the boys into monkeys.
5. Ben didn't want Sam to play football.

C. **Read the story again. Find five examples of extended sentences.**

finish up to C

Create a Character 1

People in a story are called the characters. A **character web** is a list of all the things we know about a character.

A. Here is a character web for Sam. Some of it has been done but you have to finish it.

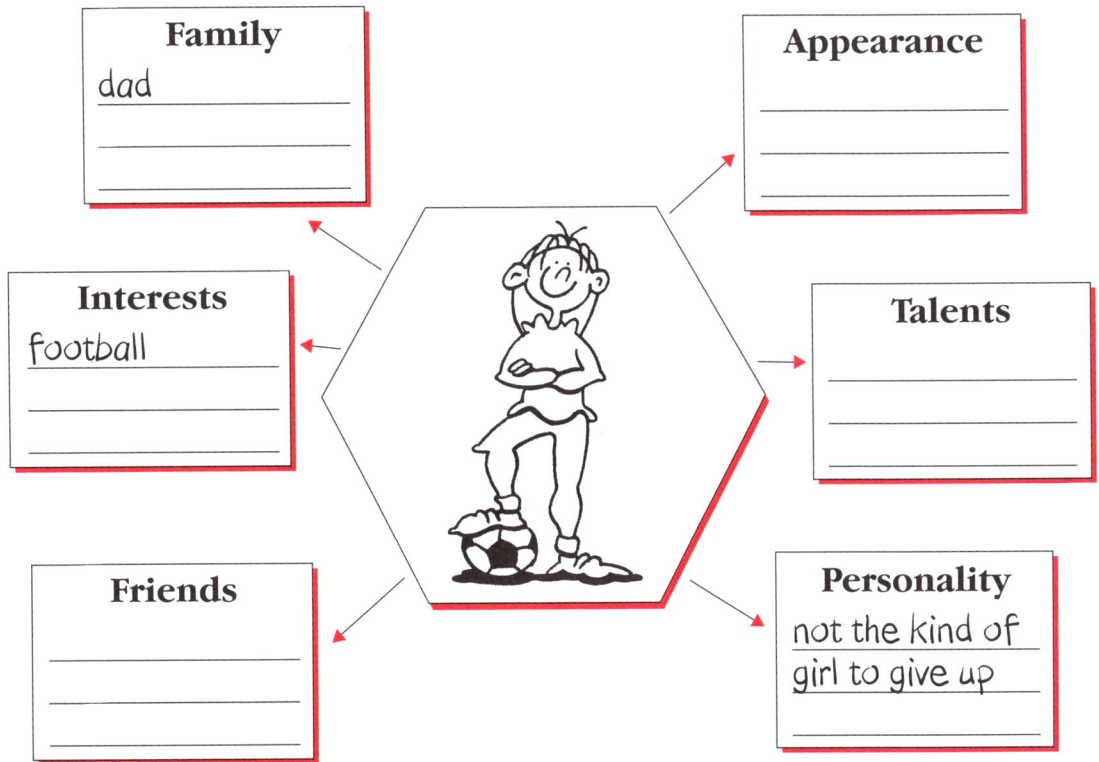

Family
dad _____
_____
_____

Appearance
_____
_____
_____

Interests
football _____
_____
_____

Talents
_____
_____
_____

Friends
_____
_____
_____

Personality
not the kind of
girl to give up
_____

B. Now describe Sam in your own words.

○ _____
○ _____
○ _____
○ _____

C. Pick one of your friends and draw a character web for him or her.

21

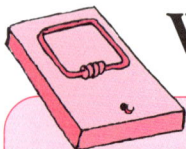

Word Trap 2

Example

I **saw** a fox last night. Have you ever **seen** one?

The pig **is** in the sty. The hens **are** in the henhouse.

I **was** at the zoo while you **were** at the circus.

A. Rewrite the sentences using the correct word.

1. "Have you _____ my books?" said my friend.

2. I _____ a great film on TV last night.

3. Where _____ the light switch in our room?

4. _____ there any sweets left in the bag?

5. I _____ watching TV last night.

6. We _____ on holidays in Spain last year.

B. Write sentences, falling into the traps on purpose. Give them to the person beside you to solve.

○ _____

○ _____

○ _____

○ _____

○ _____

Basia's Birthday Present

📖 **Before You Read:** Talk About

1. Basia is a Polish name. Where does your name come from? What does it mean?

2. This is a story about people who have been forced to leave their own country to look for a new home. Do you know what such groups are called? Why might people have to leave their own country?

📖 **After You Read:** Talk About

A. 1. Describe the place where Basia's family was resting.

2. (a) Why was Basia crying?
   (b) What reason did she give her mother?

3. (a) What objects did Basia collect?
   (b) How long did it take her to collect them?
   (c) What did she make from them?

4. What did Grandmother give her?

B. 1. What kind of person was Basia? How do we know?

2. Would you like to have been with Basia and her family in their camp? Why?

3. Was it really "hopeless"? Why?

4. Why were Basia and her family not the "worst-off refugees"?

5. What do you like most about this story? Why?

6. Tell the story from the point of view of (a) the young mother, (b) Basia's mother.

7. What do you think might have happened next?

8. Do you think that it is better to give than to receive? Why?

9. Imagine that you and your family were refugees in a foreign country. How would you like to be treated? We have many refugees in Ireland. How should we treat them? Have a class discussion.

⏩ **Moving On**

Draw a picture of the place where Basia's family were resting, based on the story. Which words would help you? List them.

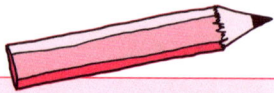

Singular and Plural 1

Remember

Nouns can be singular or plural. Usually we add **-s** or **-es** to form the plural of a noun.

Example

Singular:	cup	box
Plural:	cups	boxes

A. Add *-s* or *-es* to these words to form their plurals.

dog _____

pitch _____

beach _____

giant _____

table _____

brush _____

lake _____

rush _____

match _____

river _____

lock _____

patch _____

Not all nouns form their plurals in the same way. Look at these nouns.

Example

Singular:	lady	baby	fly
Plural:	ladies	babies	flies

B. Write the plurals of following nouns.

army _____

pony _____

country _____

fairy _____

Now look at these nouns.

Example

Singular:	life	leaf	wolf
Plural:	lives	leaves	wolves

C. Rewrite each of these sentences, changing the singular nouns to plurals.

1. The waiter put a knife and a fork on the table.

   _____

2. There was a wolf behind the bush.

   _____

3. The elf sat under the leaf.

   _____

4. The lady lit the fire with a match.

   _____

5. The thief put a ruby in his bag.

   _____

6. The army marched out of the city.

   _____

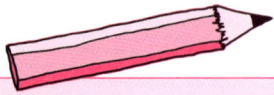

Link Words 1

Sentences can be joined using link words. These words are also called **conjunctions**.

and	**so**
or	**if**
but	**because**

Example

"Come now, sit with Grandmother **and** have some soup."

A. Use conjunctions to join these sentences.

1. Hurry up _____ you will miss the bus.

2. Ellie cried _____ Tuffy killed the bird.

3. The Great Snake's daughter wanted night to come _____ her husband could sleep.

4. Sam liked netball _____ she loved football.

5. You will fall on the slippery road _____ you don't take care.

B. Examine the story again. Find six sentences that are joined using conjunctions.

1. _____

2. _____

3. _____

4. _____

5. _____

6. _____

C. Make up sentences using the conjunctions above.

Story Planner

Read the story *Basia's Birthday Present* and complete this story planner. Talk about

- where the story happened (**setting**)
- who is in the story (**characters**)
- what happened (**problem**)
- how the story ends (**solution**)

Name of story: *Basia's Birthday Present*

Author: _____

Setting: _____

_____

_____

Characters: _____

_____

_____

Problem: _____

_____

_____

Solution: _____

_____

_____

When you are writing a story of your own, plan it using a story planner.

Writing Instructions

In the story, Basia wants to make a doll for the baby. Imagine that you want to make a gift for someone using the materials shown. Write the instructions for making your gift.

boxes

sellotape

cardboard rolls

magazines

glue

coloured paper

buttons

sticks

ribbons

I would like to make _____.

1. First _____

2. _____

3. _____

4. _____

5. _____

6. _____

7. _____

8. _____

9. _____

10. _____

Perfect Poetry 1

Read the poem *From a Railway Carriage* (page 99). Can you feel the beat or rhythm of the poem?

A. Read the poem again and clap to the rhythm.

B. Choose part of the poem and write it in the shape of a moving train.

The Caravan

Before You Read: Talk About

1. Look at the title and the illustrations. What do you think the story is about?

2. Have you ever stayed in a caravan? How is it different to living in a flat or house?

3. The family in this story has to cross the River Shannon. Read about it on page 27 of *Tyrannosaurus Sue*. Find it on a map of Ireland. What counties does it flow through?

After You Read: Talk About

A. 1. List the people in the caravan.

2. Why were the children "proud of their mother"?

3. Why was the Shark surprised?

4. What did the children use to plug the leaks?

5. Why was the flight from Dublin "futile"?

6. Why was it important to bale out the water as quickly as possible?

7. Was the horse frightened? How did Mrs Carney help him?

B. 1. Did you like this story? Why?

2. What adventures might the family have had before reaching the river?

3. Summarise the main points of the story.

4. Tell the story from the point of view of the Shark.

5. Would you like to have been in the caravan when it crossed the Shannon?

6. Why did Mrs Carney's decision seem "reckless"?

7. What kind of woman was Mrs Carney? How do we know?

▶▶ Moving On

The Carney family lived in a Traveller's caravan. What do you know about the Travellers? Find out about them by talking to a Traveller or by contacting a Traveller Association.

Dictionary Dinosaurs 2

A. **Examine the story and find the word that means:**

left behind _____

a strong flow of water _____

useless _____

load _____

soaked _____

grazing land _____

bravery _____

need _____

B. **Put the list of words in alphabetical order.**

○ 1. _____   2. _____

○ 3. _____   4. _____

○ 5. _____   6. _____

○ 7. _____   8. _____

C. **Write sentences using five of these words.**

1. _____

2. _____

3. _____

4. _____

5. _____

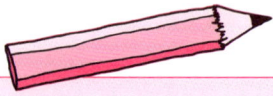

Adjectives 1

A. Read the story again. Find the adjectives that the author uses to describe these nouns.

1. a _____ moneylender

2. the _____ river

3. the _____ slipway

4. the _____ waters

5. the current was _____ and _____

6. the _____ horse

7. the _____ bank

8. a _____ shore

B. Read the story again and list other adjectives you find.

_____   _____

_____   _____

_____   _____

C. Make a class word bank of adjectives and use them when you are writing.

Tired Words 2

A. Describing something as *nice* is dull. Brainstorm other words you could use.

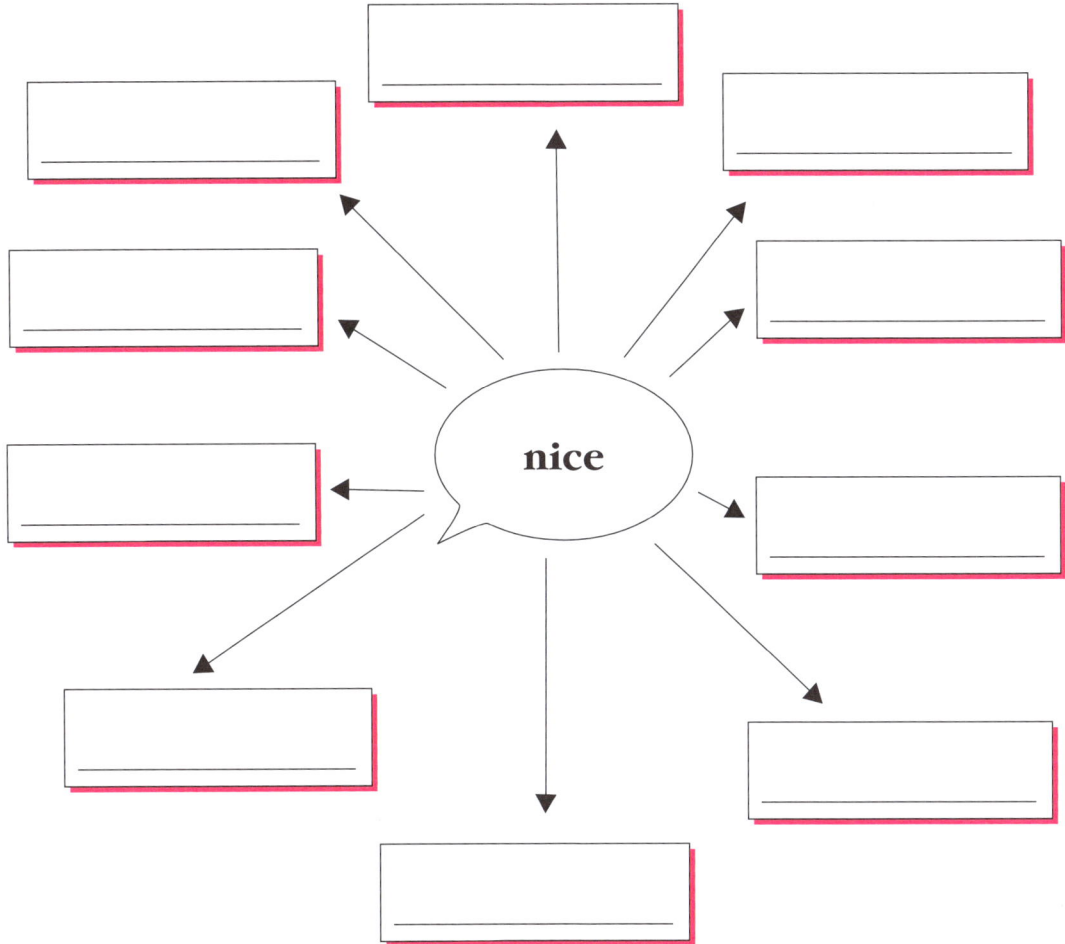

nice

Add these words to your class word bank and use them when you write.

B. Now brainstorm other words for these adjectives:

- lovely
- big
- small.

Directions

A. If someone asked you to tell them how to get from one of these towns to another, what directions would you give? Use a map of Ireland to help you.

1. From Dublin to Belfast
2. From Limerick to Cork
3. From Athlone to Sligo
4. From Dublin to Wexford
5. From Donegal Town to Galway

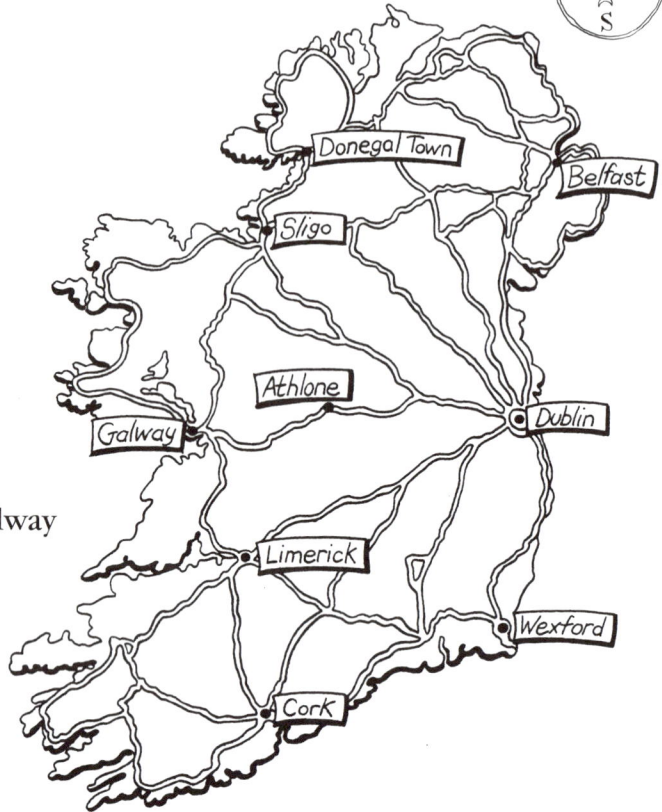

B. Write directions for getting from your home to school.

C. Now draw a map of your route.

Charlotte's Web

📖 Before You Read: Talk About

1. Look at the title of this story. What do you think the story might be about?
2. Look at the title of the chapter. What do you think the second chapter might be called?

📖 After You Read: Talk About

A. 1. (a) What was Fern's father going to do with the axe?
      (b) What did Fern try to do?
   2. What season is it in this story?
   3. Why did Fern go upstairs?
   4. What did Mr Arable do when he came into the kitchen?
   5. Why did Fern say that it was "unfair"?
   6. Why did a "queer look" come over Mr Arable's face?
   7. Why did Fern take no notice of the other children in the bus?

B. 1. What is a runt?
   2. Do you think this is a good story? Why?
   3. Were you surprised by this first chapter of the novel? Did the title give you any clue about the action?
   4. Summarise the main points of the story.
   5. Who is your favourite character? Why?
   6. What kind of man was Mr Arable? How do we know?
   7. Tell the story from the point of view of Fern's brother.
   8. Do you think it would have been right to kill the pig? Have a class debate.

▶▶ Moving On

Sometimes animals are used to describe things that people do for example, "he ate like a pig". Can you think of more examples like this? Add them to your class word bank.

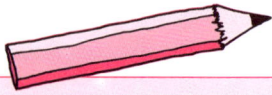

Apostrophes

Look at the title of the story. It could be written **The Web of Charlotte**. We add **'s** to show that something belongs to someone or something. This symbol ' is called an **apostrophe**.

Example

The **sneakers belonging to Fern** were sopping by the time she caught up with her father.

Fern**'s** sneakers were sopping by the time she caught up with her father.

A. Rewrite the following sentences using 's.

1. The pig belonging to Fern was called Wilbur.

   _____

2. The brother of Fern had an air rifle and a wooden knife.

   _____

3. The horse belonging to Mrs Carney was very brave.

   _____

4. The grandmother of Basia was wrapped in a heap of blankets.

   _____

5. The cap belonging to Sam didn't fool Mr Norris.

   _____

6. The daughter of the Great Snake was married to the son of the village chief.

   _____

B. Add 's to the correct word in each sentence.

1. Fern brother wanted a pig.
2. Ellie cat killed the little bird.
3. The Great Snake cave was very dark.
4. Basia present was a straw doll.
5. Sam favourite game was football.

Masculine and Feminine

A boy is male; a girl is female. A noun that names a girl is said the be **feminine**; a noun that names a boy is said to be **masculine**.

A. Match each feminine noun from the first list with a masculine noun from the second list.

mother	lord
queen	wizard
daughter	brother
lady	uncle
niece	father
aunt	nephew
witch	son
sister	king

B. Find the feminine of the following masculine nouns.

drake _____

gander _____

ram _____

husband _____

stallion _____

C. Find the masculine of the following feminine nouns.

princess _____

hen _____

vixen _____

cow _____

doe _____

Perfect Poetry 2

Read the poems *Anne and the Field-Mouse* (page 100) and *The Snare* (page 108). Think about and discuss them.

How are they alike?

_____

_____

_____

_____

How are they different?

_____

_____

_____

_____

Did you like these poems? Why?

_____

_____

_____

_____

Word Trap 3

Here are three other words we sometimes mix up.

wear	were	where

Example

I **wear** a scarf and gloves in winter.

We **were** at the seaside last weekend.

Where have you left your bucket and spade?

A. Now see if you can use them correctly.

1. Jack's blushes _____ saved by the bell.

2. "_____ _____ you yesterday?" Mr Norris asked Ben.

3. "_____ your cap pulled down real tight," said Gareth.

4. Sam stayed _____ she was.

5. Our parents like us to _____ nice clothes.

6. _____ is the Giant's Causeway?

7. You should always _____ sun-cream.

B. Now write sentences of your own.

1. (wear): _____

2. (were): _____

3. (where): _____

Weaving a Story

When we want to write about something, it is a good idea to put down our ideas first. This is called **brainstorming**. To build the story, you can then put your ideas together in a web.

A. A story web for *Charlotte's Web* might look like this. Can you complete it?

Characters

The bus

Baby pigs

school

runt

Feelings

Life at home

tears

upstairs

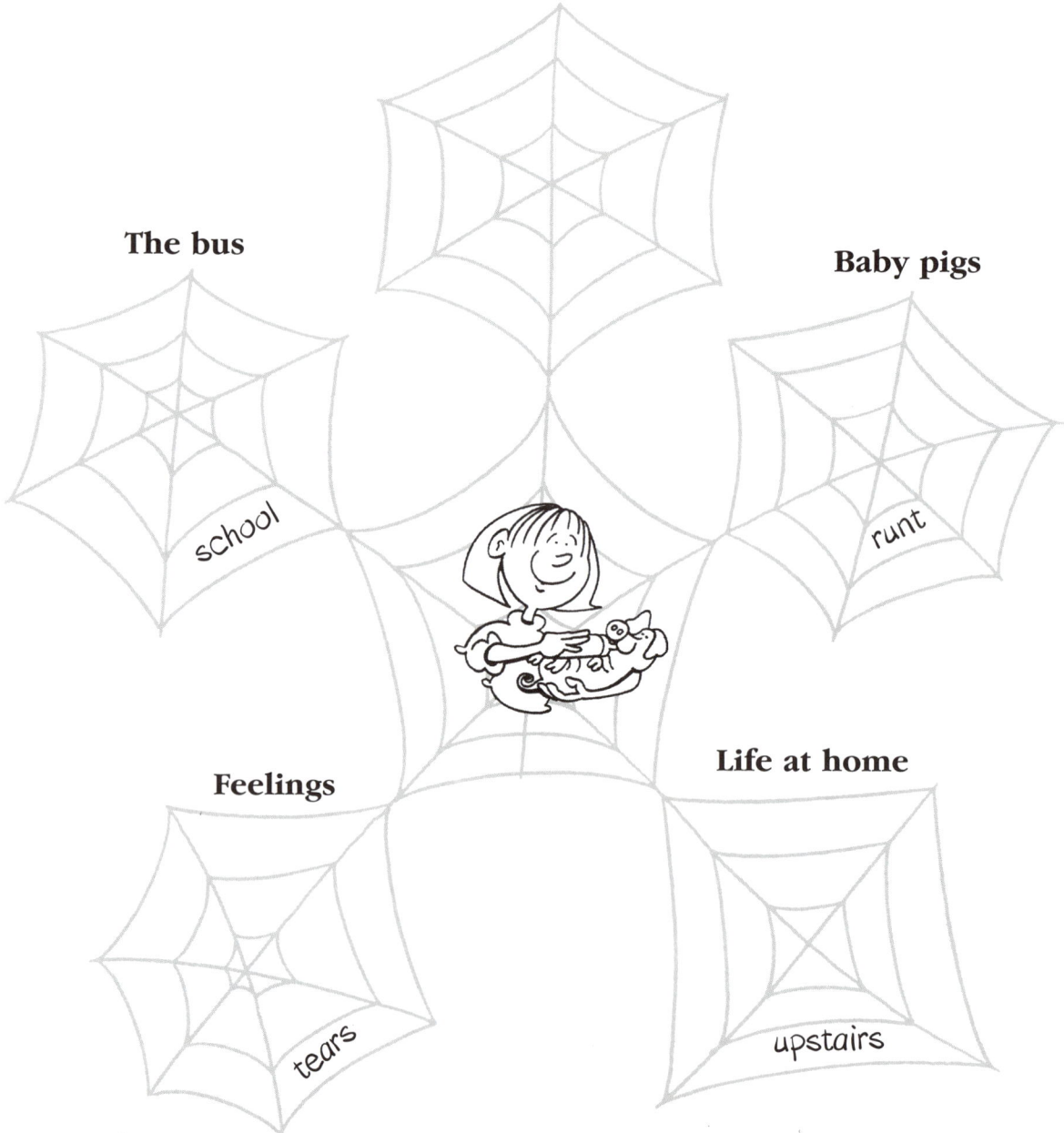

B. Choose a topic of your own. Brainstorm the topic and make a story web.

40

The Gold Cross of Killadoo

📖 Before You Read: Talk About

1. Look at the illustrations. How long ago do you think this story happened?

2. The story is set in a place called Killadoo. Many places have names that begin with Kill or Kil. List some of them. Do you know what Kill/Kil means?

3. Are there any ruins in your locality? Talk about them.

📖 After You Read: Talk About

A. 1. Who won the race to the tower?

2. How did Brother Killian know that Derval and Eoin were coming?

3. What present did Brother Killian have for the children's mother?

4. Describe Brother Cormac. What was he doing?

5. Why did Brother Cormac have a "puzzled look"?

6. Why did Brother Killian want to hide the cross?

7. Why did the children refuse to go to the tower?

B. 1. Was Derval an "impatient" girl? How do we know? Was she brave? Why?

2. Do you think that Brother Killian and Brother Cormac reached the safety of the tower? Why?

3. Would you tell your friends to read this story? Why?

4. What do you think happens next?

5. Why do you think the monastery had a high tower? Have you ever seen one of these towers? Talk about what it might have been used for.

6. Who were the Norsemen? Read about them on page 20 of *Tyrannosaurus Sue*.

▶▶ Moving On

Early Irish Christian crosses, chalices and books are decorated in a special way. Find a book in your class or library with pictures of some of them and copy one of the pictures. Write a paragraph about it.

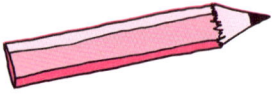

Adjectives 2

A. Read the story again. Find the adjectives that the author uses to describe these nouns.

_____	girl	_____	wall
_____	cross	_____	bees
_____	church	_____	laugh
_____	figure	_____	grass
_____	path	_____	children

B. Scan the story again and list five other adjectives.

_____   _____   _____

_____   _____

C. Write five sentences using these adjectives.

1. _____

2. _____

3. _____

4. _____

5. _____

D. Complete these sentences using suitable adjectives.

1. The _____ snake slithered through the _____ grass not wanting to be seen.

2. The _____ car sped along the _____ motorway without stopping.

3. As the _____ tree swayed in the _____ breeze, many leaves fell to the ground.

4. Michael watched as the _____ _____ squirrel gathered his _____ nuts greedily.

42

Be a Reporter 1

Today you are a reporter for the school newspaper. Your job is to interview Brother Killian. Read the story again and write down the questions you want to ask. Find a partner to be Brother Killian and ask the questions.

1. _____

2. _____

3. _____

4. _____

5. _____

6. _____

7. _____

8. _____

9. _____

10. _____

Word Dominoes

Here is a set of word dominoes. The last part of one word becomes the first of the next. Can you think of words to complete the other pairs of dominoes?

bus	lane

lane	way

The Story of Tracy Beaker

Before You Read: Talk About

1. Do you keep a diary of the things that happen to you from day to day?

2. Look at the illustrations. Do you think Tracy is happy or unhappy? Why do you think so?

3. List ten words that you think might be in the story.

After You Read: Talk About

A. 1. (a) What age is Tracy Beaker?
   (b) What date is her birthday?
   (c) Who else has a birthday on this day?

2. (a) Why did Tracy have only "half a wish"?
   (b) Does she believe in wishes? Why?

3. (a) List some of the things about Tracy that we know.
   (b) List some of the things that we don't know.

4. Why would Tracy fancy being a witch?

5. What is the name of Tracy's teacher?

6. Does Tracy have a best friend? How do we know?

7. Why would Tracy like a Rottweiler?

B. 1. Did you like this story? Why?

2. Do you like Tracy? Why?

3. Why is Tracy a "little titch"?

4. Do you think Tracy is happy at her children's home? How do we know?

5. Imagine you are Camilla. What would you say about Tracy?

6. Tracy has the same birthday as Peter. Do you share your birthday with anyone you know? Find out if you have the same birthday as someone famous.

▶▶ Moving On

What do you imagine life will be like in 2091? Draw a picture.

Be a Publisher

Using Tracy Beaker's book as a guide, make your own book about yourself. Don't forget to add lots of drawings and pictures to your book. Why not design an interesting cover when you have finished?

Page 1

Write about your name, age, birthday and where you were born. Why not use a stamp pad to print your fingerprints?

Page 2

Write about how tall you are, what you weigh, what kind of eyes you have and your hair.

Page 3

Write about things that have happened to you at school.

Page 4

Write about your lucky number, your favourite colour, your best friend and what you like to eat.

Page 5

Write about your favourite things and also about things you don't like.

Contractions

Remember

Sometimes we take short-cuts in writing. We leave out a letter or letters and make one word out of two. This is called a _____.

Do you remember what this symbol means: ' ? An apostrophe is also used to show where letters have been left out.

Examples

did + **not** = **didn't**   **I** + **will** = **I'll**

A. Examine the story again and list all the contractions you find.

- ○ _____   _____
- ○ _____   _____
- ○ _____   _____
- ○ _____   _____

B. Now see if you can write them as two separate words.

- ○ _____   _____
- ○ _____   _____
- ○ _____   _____
- ○ _____   _____

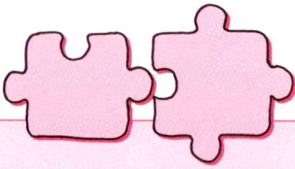

Word Magic 1

When letters such as as **un-** or **dis-** are placed at the beginning of a word, they change its meaning. These letters are called a **prefix**.

Example

happy	**un**happy
like	**dis**like

A. Choose one of the prefixes and give each word its opposite meaning.

kind _____   sure _____

appear _____   agree _____

advantage _____   fair _____

B. Write six sentences using these new words.

1. _____

2. _____

3. _____

4. _____

5. _____

6. _____

C. Write each sentence, using a suitable word from this list.

unwise	disliked	disagreed	unsure

1. It was _____ of Tuffy to kill the cat.

2. Mrs Carney was _____ whether the caravan could cross the river.

3. Ben _____ with Gareth that Sam should play football.

4. Tracy Beaker _____ Camilla.

48

Be a Critic

Your class has been asked to perform a play at school assembly next week. You have to choose between *Telling Tales* (page 127) or *Abducted by Aliens* (page 141).

I choose _____

Author: _____

I liked this play because

_____

_____

_____

What we need to do now to get ready:

_____

_____

_____

_____

_____

_____

_____

_____

When the VR-Bookatron Went Wrong

Before You Read: Talk About

1. Look at the title. What do you think the letters "VR" stand for? What do you think a "Bookatron" is? (Clue: Look at the first four letters before you answer.)

2. Do you know the story of *The Wizard of Oz*? Have you seen the film? Name the main characters and briefly retell the story.

After You Read: Talk About

A. 1. (a) What did Carrie want for her birthday?
   (b) What did she receive? Describe her present.

2. (a) Why did people use Bookatrons?
   (b) How did a Bookatron work?

3. List some of Carrie's favourite books.

4. Why did Carrie press Option number 5?

5. What did Carrie want from the Wizard of Oz?

6. (a) List some of the nasty things Paul did to Carrie.
   (b) Why did Carrie's parents not believe her when she complained?

B. 1. What do you think happens next in the story?

2. Summarise the main points of the story.

3. Would you like a Bookatron? Why?

4. What words tell you that Carrie was disappointed in her present?

5. How many years from now do you think this story is set?

6. In the story people have become too lazy to read actual books. Do you think this will ever happen some day? How would you feel if it did?

Moving On

If you could invent a machine to do anything, what would you choose for it to do? Describe your machine. Draw and label it.

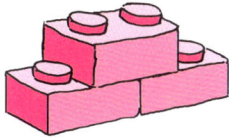

Dictionary Dinosaurs 3

A. Here is a list of words from *When the VR-Bookatron Went Wrong*. Find the meanings in your dictionary and write them down.

scanned _____

beamed _____

shimmered _____

timidly _____

cyclone _____

cowardly _____

vanished _____

scowled _____

modern _____

inserted _____

B. Put the list of words in alphabetical order.

1. _____   2. _____

3. _____   4. _____

5. _____   6. _____

7. _____   8. _____

9. _____   10. _____

C. Write sentences using five of these words.

1. _____

2. _____

3. _____

4. _____

5. _____

Homonyms

Some words sound the same but look different. They are called **homonyms**. They sound the same but do not have the same meaning.

Example

flour   flower

A. Match the words from the first list that sound the same as words from the second list.

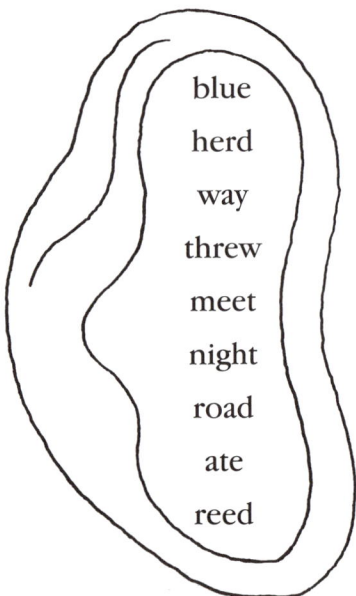

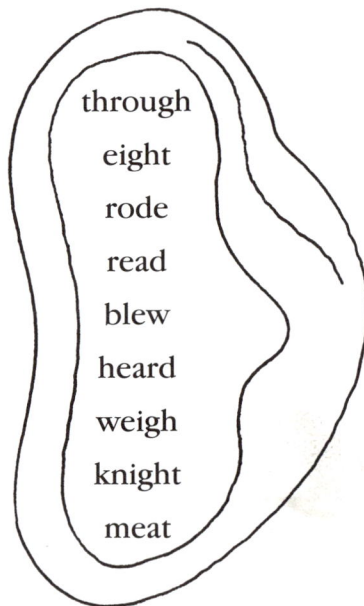

blue	through
herd	eight
way	rode
threw	read
meet	blew
night	heard
road	weigh
ate	knight
reed	meat

B. Choose a word from each pair. Draw a picture to describe it and give it to the person beside you to solve.

C. Complete these sentences using words from the list.

1. On the _____ to the check-out, I stopped to _____ some fruit.

2. Dad asked me to _____ him at the _____ counter in the shop.

3. The brave _____ galloped through the dark _____.

4. The man _____ his dinner at _____ o'clock.

D. Examine the story again. List all the homonyms you find.

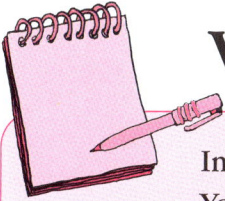

What Happens Next?

Imagine you receive a VR-Bookatron as a birthday present.
You insert your favourite book into the Bookatron. List the viewpoint options. Which option would you choose? What do you think might happen?

Viewpoint options

1. _____

2. _____

3. _____

4. _____

Selected option

_____

What happens next?

_____

_____

_____

_____

_____

_____

Perfect Poetry 3

A. Bullies can hurt people in many ways; by their actions and their words. Read the poem *Truth* (page 115) and brainstorm some of the things that could hurt you.

B. Sometimes the things that people say can make you feel sad, happy or even angry. List some feeling words for these word banks.

Sad

Angry

Happy

Liza's Lamb

📖 **Before You Read:** Talk About

1. Look at the title. What do you think the story is about?

2. Look at the chapter title and the introduction. What do you think the story is about now?

3. Have you ever tried to use a wheelchair? Do you think it would be difficult?

📖 **After You Read:** Talk About

A. 1. Why do you think Shane's arms got tired?

2. What games or equipment were in the playroom? List them.

3. What did Shane see while standing with Da one morning?

4. (a) What day of the week was it?
   (b) On what day would Shane go home?

5. Was Shane really sleeping? What was he doing?

B. 1. Why did Shane feel like the sixth lamb?

2. What did Shane tell Liza about what he had done in the playroom? Was he telling the truth?

3. Why did Shane feel bad when he looked at Liza's hunched figure in the bed? Why had Liza turned away from him?

4. Which of the two children do you think has the larger family? Why?

5. Why did Shane "hate" Dublin?

6. Summarise the main points of the story.

7. What do you think happens next in the story?

8. Tell the story from the point of view of (a) Liza, (b) Liza's mammy.

9. What do you like best about this story? Why?

▶▶ **Moving On**

Do you know anyone who is in hospital? Design a get well soon card or postcard to send to them.

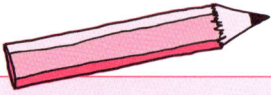

Commas

Commas are used to break up two parts of a sentence. We pause slightly at a comma when we read.

Commas are also used to break up lists of words.

A. Examine the story again and rewrite these sentences adding commas.

1. It was great even though it was much harder to use than he thought it would be.

2. Once he had to swerve to avoid another boy in a wheelchair coming the other way.

3. This evening he'd cross off Saturday.

4. The boy didn't know anything Shane thought.

5. She was younger than Mammy but she looked nice.

6. It wasn't as easy as it looked on the television especially when you were in a wheelchair and he felt like an idiot.

B. Now try these.

1. My name is Tracy Beaker I'm ten years old.

2. As Tracy cut the cake Peter cut it too.

3. When she was in the hospital she cried a lot.

4. As she measured her height the ruler kept on wobbling.

5. Using Adele's make-up she turned herself into an incredible vampire.

6. Tracy liked Mars Bars popcorn Big Macs and jelly spiders.

Feelings

A. Faces often show how people feel. Imagine how Shane and Liza felt in hospital. Draw their faces.

Shane	**Liza**

B. Read the story again and list as many words as you can that show how Shane and Liza felt.

Shane	Liza

Making Lists

A. Sometimes we make lists to help us remember things. Complete these lists to help you remember the stories you have already read. Write each list in alphabetical order.

South American creatures

Character names

Animals that live in Ireland

_____
_____
_____
_____
_____
_____
_____
_____
_____
_____
_____

A list of your choice

_____
_____
_____
_____
_____
_____
_____
_____
_____
_____
_____
_____
_____
_____
_____

B. Write sentences, using four words from the lists above in each one.
Don't forget to use commas!

1. _____

2. _____

3. _____

4. _____

Timetable

When someone is in hospital, their day follows a strict timetable. Draw up Liza's timetable for a day in hospital.

TIME		TIME	
6.00	wake-up call	14.00	
6.30		14.30	
7.00		15.00	
7.30		15.30	
8.00		16.00	visiting time
8.30		16.30	
9.00		17.00	
9.30		17.30	
10.00		18.00	
10.30		18.30	
11.00		19.00	
11.30		19.30	
12.00		20.00	
12.30		20.30	
13.00		21.00	lights out
13.30			

Dear Norman

Before You Read: *Talk About*

1. Look at the title. What do you think the story is about?
2. Read the first letter. What do you think it is about now?
3. What do you think will happen next?
4. Did you ever think about running away from home? Talk about it.

After You Read: *Talk About*

A. 1. Why do you think Norman ran away from home?
   2. Why did Norman leave through the back door?
   3. List what you think Norman might have brought with him when he moved to the tree house.
   4. What skills will Norman need for "his life in the wild"?
   5. A repairman has called to Norman's home. Why?
   6. (a) List some of the articles featured in *Good Boy* magazine.
      (b) What will Norman receive if he orders the magazine?

B. 1. Norman's Mum mentions some things which might make living in a tree house not very nice. What are these? Do you think that Norman will have thought of them? Why?
   2. Why do you think Daniel Barleycorn wrote to Norman?
   3. Were Norman's parents understanding? What sentences in the story give you the clue?
   4. Does Eileen like Norman's sister? How do we know?
   5. Why do you think Norman decided to move back home?
   6. Do you think this is an amusing story? Why?
   7. Tell the story from the point of view of Norman's sister Beth.
   8. Would you like to live in a tree house? Why?

▶▶ Moving On

Draw the outline of an envelope and address it to a friend or pen pal.

Lovely Letters

Read the first two letters in **_Dear Norman_** from his Mum and Dad.
Imagine the letter Norman wrote in reply and write it below.

Remember

Don't forget to include the following:
- address
- date
- _Dear_ ...
- signed

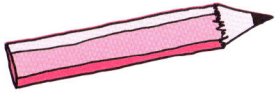

Singular and Plural 2

A. Write the plurals of the following nouns.

life _____   wish _____

sandwich _____   photograph _____

territory _____   cloth _____

Not all nouns form their plurals in the same way. Look at these nouns.

Example

Singular:	man	goose	mouse
Plural:	men	geese	mice

B. Now write the plurals of these nouns.

woman _____   tooth _____

louse _____   foot _____

Some nouns do not change at all in the plural.

Example

Singular:	fish	deer
Plural:	fish	deer

C. Now write the plural of these nouns.

dormouse _____   trout _____

bus _____   branch _____

child _____   cod _____

torch _____   paw _____

Friendly Advice

Mrs Bouquet could see that Norman did not need to know geography, history or music in the tree house. He did, however, need "skills useful for life in the wild". Offer some advice to Norman on the skills he needs in his new life and write him a letter. Don't forget to address and sign it!

Be a Reporter 2

You are a reporter for a local newspaper. You have been asked to write a report about the boy in the tree house. List ten questions that you would ask Norman and then write your report.

1. _____
2. _____
3. _____
4. _____
5. _____
6. _____
7. _____
8. _____
9. _____
10. _____

_____
_____
_____
_____
_____
_____
_____
_____

Harry Potter and the Philosopher's Stone

Before You Read: Talk About

1. Look at the title. Who is Harry Potter?

2. Look up the word "philosopher" in your dictionary. What do you imagine the "philosopher's stone" is?

3. List some of the Harry Potter novels. Do you like them? Why?

After You Read: Talk About

A. 1. (a) What was the address of the Dursleys?
   (b) How long had Harry Potter lived with them?

2. Why did Harry find a spider in his socks?

3. Why did Harry's aunt say that she would buy two more presents for Dudley?

4. Describe Dudley.

B. 1. What was the "first rule for a quiet life with the Dursley's"? Why do you think this was so?

2. What kind of person is Harry Potter? Do you like him? Why?

3. In what way was Dudley "just like his father"?

4. Do you think Harry's aunt and uncle treat him fairly? What in the story tells you about this?

5. What do you think happens next in the story?

6. Summarise the main points of the story.

7. Tell the story from the point of view of Dudley.

▶▶ Moving On

Make a series of cartoon drawings of Dudley Dursley based on the descriptions of the photos on the mantlepiece.

Amazing Acrostics

A. Make a Harry Potter acrostic. Add a sentence for each letter.

Harry Potter lives with his aunt, uncle and cousin.	
A	
R	
R	
Y	
P	
O	
T	
T	
E	
R	

B. Write an acrostic for another character you have read about.

Extending a Sentence 2

Example

Nearly ten years passed since the Dursleys had woken up to find their nephew on the front step, **but** Privet Drive had hardly changed at all.

A. Here is a list of conjunctions. Examine the story and list sentences from the story that contain these conjunctions.

and	but	because
which	unless	as

1. _____

2. _____

3. _____

4. _____

5. _____

6. _____

7. _____

8. _____

9. _____

10. _____

B. Now use each conjunction in a sentence of your own.

Book Invitation

A. What is the best book you have ever read? Invite a friend to read the book by filling in the invitation below.

Invitation

_____

is invited to read

_____

because

_____

_____

_____

_____

Enjoy your read!

B. Make invitation cards for other books you have read and display them in your class or school library.

C. You have been asked by a publishing company to design a book cover for *Harry Potter and the Philosopher's Stone*. Create your own design. Look at page 18 of *Tyrannosaurus Sue* to see what you should include.

Redraft and Edit 1

When we write we must always check over what we have done and correct our mistakes. This is called **editing**.

Redraft and edit this piece from *Harry Potter and the Philosopher's Stone*. Don't look at your book until you have finished.

purhaps it has something two do with living in a cuboard, but Harry had

always bin small and skinny four his age he looked even smaller then he really

wuz because all he had too were wear old cloths of Dudley's and Dudley was

about for times bigger than he were. Harryhad a thin face knobly knees black

hair and brite-green eyes he wore round glasses held together with a lott of

Sellotape because of all the times Dudley had punched him on the nose

Final draft

70

Matilda

Before You Read: Talk About

1. *Matilda* is a Roald Dahl story. What other Roald Dahl stories do you know?

2. Look at the pictures. What clues do they give you about the story?

3. Have you seen any films of the stories of Roald Dahl? Talk about your favourite.

After You Read: Talk About

A. 1. (a) What age was Matilda when she started school?
      (b) What age were most other children?

   2. Describe the village school.

   3. Were Matilda's parents concerned about her education?

   4. What will the children be expected to know
      (a) by the end of the week, (b) in a year's time?

B. 1. Would you like to have been in this school? Why?

   2. Why was Matilda's teacher "considerably shaken" after their conversation?

   3. What kind of person was Miss Honey? Did her name suit her? Why? List some of the words used to describe her.

   4. What kind of person was Miss Trunchbull? List some of the words used to describe her.

   5. Do you think there really could be a teacher as wicked as Miss Trunchbull? Explain why you think so.

   6. Who do you think taught Matilda her tables? How did she learn them? Do you think she was very clever? Why?

   7. Tell the story from the point of view of Matilda's teacher.

   8. What do you think happened next?

▶▶ Moving On

Select any one of Roald Dahl's characters. Pretend that you are that person and write a personal profile.

Create a Character 2

A. Do you remember how to build a character web? Look again at page 21. Now build character webs for Harry and Matilda.

B. Imagine that one day Harry and Matilda met! What questions might they ask each other? Write some of them here.

Harry's questions

Matilda's questions

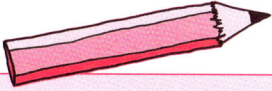

Past and Present 2

Not every verb in the past tense ends in -ed.

Example

Past tense: Miss Jennifer Honey **was** a mild and quiet person who never raised her voice.

Present tense: Miss Jennifer Honey **is** a mild and quiet person who never raises her voice.

A. Match the following present tense verbs to their past tenses.

is	sank
have	flew
run	grew
fly	had
go	ran
sink	bought
grow	was
buy	made
make	went

B. Now write these sentences in the past tense.

1. In the zoo, I see monkeys and hear lions roaring.
2. I think it is going to rain.
3. The police come and catch the burglars.
4. The woman sings in the talent competition and wins.
5. I write to my pen-pal every week.
6. "I am very happy that I have a new car," says Mum.

C. Examine the first page of the story and list all the verbs you find that are in the past tense.

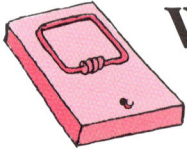

Word Trap 4

Write sentences using each of these words correctly.

1. (saw): _____
2. (seen): _____
3. (is): _____
4. (are): _____
5. (was): _____
6. (were): _____
7. (wear): _____
8. (were): _____
9. (where): _____
10. (our): _____
11. (of): _____
12. (off): _____
13. (their): _____
14. (there): _____
15. (to): _____
16. (two): _____
17. (too): _____

74

Agree or Disagree

Sometimes when we have a discussion we do not always agree with each other. We should be able to give reasons.

In the story *Matilda*, Miss Honey tells the children that in a year's time they should know their multiplication tables up to twelve. Do we need to learn them? What use are they to us? List five reasons why you agree and five reasons why you disagree with Miss Honey.

I agree because …	I disagree because …
1.	1.
2.	2.
3.	3.
4.	4.
5.	5.

Alice in Wonderland

📖 Before You Read: Talk About

1. Look at the title. Have you heard of this story before?

2. Look at the chapter title and the pictures. What do you think happens to Alice?

3. Do you know any other stories where characters end up in magical or fantasy lands? List them and talk about what happens in each.

📖 After You Read: Talk About

A. 1. (a) What did Alice see while she was sitting on the bank?
     (b) What was "remarkable" about it?

2. (a) Why did Alice "not like to drop the jar"?
     (b) What did she do with it?

3. What was the name of Alice's cat?

4. Why did Alice run after the Rabbit? Would you have done that? Why?

5. Did Alice hurt herself when she fell down the well? Why?

B. 1. Tell the story from the point of view of the Rabbit.

2. What do you think happens next?

3. Do you think that the events in this story really took place?

4. Is Alice an "ignorant little girl"? Is she a polite little girl? Do you like her?

5. Did you like this story? Why?

6. Summarise the main points of the story.

7. Do you know what "latitude" and "longitude" are?

▶▶ Moving On

What do you imagine were in all the cupboards that Alice passed by?
Can you draw or make a collage picture of one of them and include some interesting things.

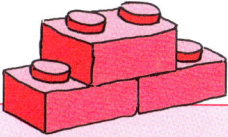

Collective Nouns

A **collective noun** is the name given to a group of people or things.

Example

one whale   a **school** of whales

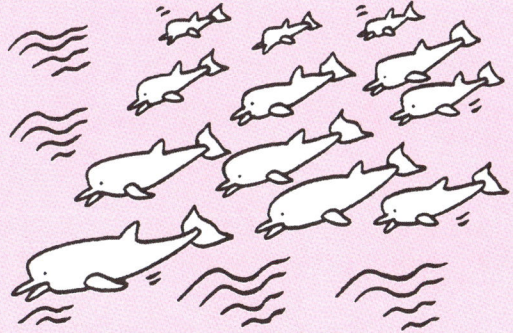

A. Choose a suitable collective noun for each of these.

| litter | pride | pack | gaggle | herd | flock |

A _____ of cows

A _____ of geese

A _____ of lions

A _____ of puppies

A _____ of sheep

A _____ of wolves

B. Add a noun to each of the following.

A shoal of _____

A swarm of _____

A crowd of _____

A flotilla of _____

A nest of _____

A bunch of _____

C. Complete the following sentences.

1. A _____ of buffalo charged the hunter.

2. The leopard defended her litter of _____.

3. The children bought Mum a _____ of flowers.

4. Babe made friends with the flock of _____.

5. The _____ of whales surrounded the shoal of _____.

6. Even a pride of _____ is afraid of a _____ of elephants.

Verbs and Adverbs

A word can be used to describe a verb. This word is called an **adverb**.

Example

The girl walked **slowly** along the road.

A. Complete these sentences, adding *-ly* or *-ily* to the word in brackets.

1. Mr Morris lifted Sam's cap _____ off her head. (gentle)

2. Basia thought to herself _____. (quiet)

3. The wheels of the caravan sank _____ into the water. (slow)

4. Derval muttered _____ to herself. (fierce)

5. Avery was _____ armed. (heavy)

6. Cormac _____ polished the gold cross. (busy)

B. Match the verbs to the adverbs.

yelled	sadly
ate	happily
walked	crossly
wrote	ravenously
laughed	neatly
cried	awkwardly
stamped	greedily
snatched	angrily

C. Examine the story again. Find as many adverbs as you can and use five of them in sentences.

Redraft and Edit 2

Redraft and edit this piece from *Alice in Wonderland*. Don't look at your book until you have finished.

well thought Alice two herself after such a fall as this i shall think nuthing of

_____

tumbling downstairs how brave they'll all think me at home why i wouldn't say

_____

anything about it even if i fell of the top off the house

_____

downdown down would the fall never come to an end i wonder how many

_____

miles i've fallen this time she said aloud i must be getting somewhere near the

_____

centre of the earth let me see that would be for thousand miles down i think …

_____

Final draft _____

_____

_____

_____

_____

_____

_____

_____

_____

_____

Table of Contents

Most books have a **table of contents**. It tells you what the different chapters of a book are, as well as the page number on which each chapter begins. Look at the table of contents and answer the following questions.

Table of Contents

1. What is the book about?

   _____

2. How many chapters are there in the book?

   _____

3. Which chapter begins on page 39?

   _____

4. On what page does the chapter about the caterpillar begin?

   _____

5. What chapter tells you about pigs?

   _____

6. What would you read about on page 51?

   _____

7. What would you read about on page 6?

   _____

Lively Limericks

Read Michael Palin's *Limericks* (page 122). Can you see and hear a pattern?

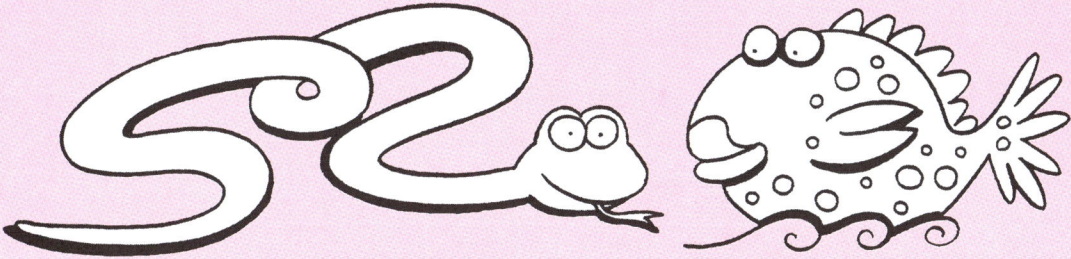

A. Now make up your own limericks.

There was a young lady from Spain

_____

_____

_____

_____

There once was a man from Japan

_____

_____

_____

_____

B. Read your limericks aloud to your classmates.

The Táin

Before You Read: *Talk About*

1. This tale is based on one of the most famous stories from Irish folklore. Do you know any other such stories? Can you retell one?

2. Find (a) Cruachán, (b) Cooley on a map of Ireland.

After You Read: *Talk About*

A.
1. When did the trouble begin?
2. Where did the Warrior Queen live?
3. Why did she and her husband quarrel?
4. How did they decide to settle the quarrel?
5. List all their possessions.

B.
1. Why was Maeve called the "Warrior Queen"?
2. What kind of man was Ailill? Why?
3. What do you think happens next in the story?
4. Did you like this story? Why?
5. Would you like to be one of Maeve's servants? Why?
6. Tell the story from the point of view of (a) the Chief Messenger, (b) the owner of the Brown Bull.
7. Was the mission "successful"? What happened?
8. Do you think Daire was right to refuse to lend the Brown Bull? Why?
9. Do you think it was right for the Queen to take the Brown Bull by force? Why?

▶▶ **Moving On**

Write a list of famous Irish story characters and put them into a word search grid. Fill the blank spaces with other letters and give your word search to the person beside you to solve.

Dictionary Dinosaurs 4

A. Examine the story and find the word that means:

loved very much _____

very calm _____

anger, irritation _____

very angry _____

shining brightly _____

unending _____

nervously _____

object, aim _____

B. Put the list of words in alphabetical order.

1. _____   2. _____

3. _____   4. _____

5. _____   6. _____

7. _____   8. _____

C. Write sentences using five of these words.

1. _____

2. _____

3. _____

4. _____

5. _____

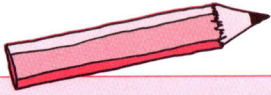

Word Sorting

A noun is _____.

An adjective is _____.

A verb is _____.

An adverb is _____.

A. The author of *The Táin* needs your help to sort out these words into nouns, adjectives, verbs and adverbs.

furiously	walk	woke	sing	beautiful
smiled	Maeve	sweet	lovely	immediately
quarrelled	breeze	playful	heatedly	went
proud	murmuring	bees	night	angrily
summer	drowsy	handsomely	combed	hair
anxiously	face	Ailill	little	pleasantly

Nouns	Adjectives	Verbs	Adverbs

B. Choose five words from the lists above and put them into sentences.

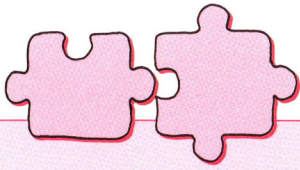

Word Magic 2

Example

fortune	**mis**fortune
slip	**non**-slip

A. Add the correct prefixes to these words to make their opposites.

_____ stick   _____ placed

_____ print   _____ appeared

_____ friendly   _____ laid

_____ behave   _____ sense

_____ smoker   _____ understand

B. Complete the following sentences using words from the list above.

1. Dad _____ the car keys.

2. The children in the yard were _____ to the new boy.

3. Mum used a _____ pan to fry the eggs.

4. A _____ does not like the smell of cigarettes.

5. Our teacher is not pleased if we _____.

6. Tuffy thought the fuss about the dead bird was _____.

7. I found a _____ in the newspaper.

8. The magician _____ at the end of his trick.

C. Write six sentences using these new words.

Sound Snatch

Some of the words from *The Táin* have got mixed up. Can you sort the syllables?
Use your book to help you.

Words with two syllables

gar gan
chief
vants les
ing
pal sing
tain ser
den
be
son ace

Words with three syllables

for ing to als
mur er her
get ful
at what
an mur
got
ed tract ten
ev beau
im ti

The Selfish Giant

Before You Read: Talk About

1. Look at the title. What do you think the story is about?
2. Read the first paragraph of the story. What do you think happens next?
3. This story was written by a famous Irish writer called Oscar Wilde. Do you know where there is a statue of him? (Clue: A park in Dublin.)

After You Read: Talk About

A. 1. (a) Where had the Giant been?
   (b) How long had he spent there?
   2. (a) What did the Giant say?
   (b) What did the Giant do?
   3. What did the "beautiful flower" do? Why?
   4. What happened one morning?
   5. Why was it still winter in one corner of the garden? What happened there?
   6. What happened when the Giant went into the garden?
   7. Why did the little boy not run away?

B. 1. Do you think the Giant's conversation was "limited"? Why?
   2. What "marvellous thing" happened one winter morning?
   3. (a) What marks were on the child's hands and feet?
   (b) Who do you think the child was?
   4. Do you think this is a sad story? Why?
   5. Did you like the Giant? Why?
   6. (a) Why do you think Spring never arrived in the Giant's garden?
   (b) Why do you think it eventually returned?

Moving On

Can you picture the characters of the Snow, Frost, Hail and North Wind? What colours would you use? Paint them.

Picture This!

Examine the story again and find words to place in these shapes.

Spring words

Summer words

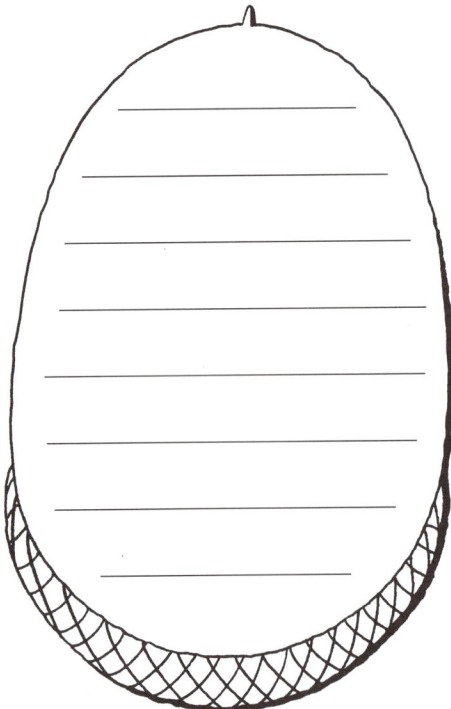

Autumn words

Winter words

Responding to a Character

Read the story again and think about the character of the giant. How did you feel about him at the beginning of the story and how did you feel about him at the end?

I felt about the giant …	
at the beginning	**at the end**

Compare your responses with the person beside you.

Developing a Character

What do you think each of these seasonal characters would look like? Draw a picture and write a short character profile for each.

Sir Winter

Sir Spring

Sir Summer

Sir Autumn

Quiztime!

A. Here is a short quiz about *Giants, Fishbones and Chocolate*. Answer the questions and compare your answers with the person beside you.

1. What did the sign on the wall of the Giant's Garden say?
2. What was the younger Monk's name?
3. Why did Miss Brown get narked?
4. What was the name of the nurse from Mayo?
5. Whose story ended up in the newspaper the wrong way round?
6. What was the name of the moneylender?
7. Who found a black mamba?
8. Who had a funeral on Tuesday?
9. Name two characters who were very fond of chewing gum?
10. What was the name of the head teacher at Matilda's school?
11. What was the name of the football coach?
12. What is Tracy Beaker's favourite colour?
13. Who invited Norman to a birthday party?
14. What country was Basia from?
15. What was Fern's surname?
16. Where did Maeve build her palace?
17. What was in the jar that Alice took off the shelf?
18. Who lived on the banks of the River Amazon?
19. Name Harry's aunt, uncle and cousin.
20. Who wrote *The Wizard of Oz?*

B. Why not make up your own quiz based on the stories and give your questions to the person beside you to answer?

Little Red Riding Hood: The Wolf's Story

Before You Read: Talk About

1. Look at the title. What do you think the story is about?

2. Retell the original story of *Little Red Riding Hood*.

3. Read the first paragraph of the story. Why does the wolf want to set the record straight?

4. Why do you think the wolf is always seen as wicked? Are there other creatures with bad reputations?

After You Read: Talk About

A. 1. What was the "first lie"?

2. Why did the wolf think that it wasn't "so terrible" to eat Red Riding Hood?

3. Why do you think the wolf didn't eat Red Riding Hood when they met in the wood? What reason does the wolf give?

4. Why might the wolf not like screams?

5. Why didn't the wolf make a "run for it"?

B. 1. Do you believe the wolf's version of the story?

2. Why did the wolf "stay under the covers" when Red Riding Hood entered the cottage?

3. Was Granny really a "tough old bird"?

4. List the things that Granny didn't want the reporters to know.

5. Did you find this story amusing? Why?

6. Summarise the main points of the story.

7. Tell the story from the point of view of Granny.

Moving On

Make a small drama of a court scene at which the wolf is being tried.

Paragraphs

A **paragraph** is a group of sentences dealing with the same idea. The first word of a paragraph usually starts a little way in from the margin.

Read the story *Jack and the Beanstalk*. What happens to the giant? Now tell the story as the giant might like to tell it. The words in the box will help you.

Helpful words

- unfair
- gentle
- generous
- magic beans
- friendly
- wouldn't hurt a fly
- poor and hungry

Paragraph 1: The giant didn't really want to kill Jack. He just wanted to help Jack and his mother.

Paragraph 2: Jack stole the hen that laid golden eggs, bags of money and a singing harp from the giant. The giant wanted to give these things to Jack and lots more besides.

Paragraph 3: The giant runs after Jack to tell him all these things.

Paragraph 4: What happens? What does the giant say?

Be a Costume Designer

Your class has been asked to perform *Roald Dahl's Charlie and the Chocolate Factory* (page 131) at a school concert. Read the play and design costumes for the characters using pictures and words.

Willy Wonka _____

_____

_____

_____

_____

Violet _____

_____

_____

_____

_____

Mike _____

_____

_____

_____

_____

_____

Veruca _____

_____

_____

_____

_____

_____

Mrs Beauregarde _____

_____

_____

_____

_____

_____

Mr Salt _____

_____

_____

_____

_____

_____

Charlie _____

_____

_____

_____

_____

Oompa-Loompa _____

_____

_____

_____

_____

Perfect Poetry 4

My favourite poem: _____

Poet: _____

I liked this poem because _____

_____

_____

_____

Words I liked in this poem: _____

_____

_____

_____

It made me feel _____

_____

_____

_____

What I would like to say to the poet: _____

_____

_____

_____

_____

Signed: _____   Date _____

Personal Opinions

There are many different stories in the book. Perhaps you liked some and didn't like others. How did they make you feel?

I liked

_____

_____

_____

I did not like

_____

_____

_____

Characters I liked

_____

_____

Characters I did not like

_____

_____

_____

I felt

_____

_____

_____